Mujeres, The Magic,
The Movement and The Muse:

An Anthology of Women Writers

Peggy Robles-Alvarado

Mujeres, The Magic,
The Movement, and The Muse:
An Anthology of Women Writers

ISBN: 978-0-9832777-3-6
Concept and editing by Peggy Robles-Alvarado
Cover Art by Nia Andino
Cover and Layout by Carmelo Dominguez - vginyc.com
Proofreading and additional edits by Nia Andino,
Yoseli Castillo Fuertes and Janel Cloyd

This publication is made possible by Robleswrites Productions
and this project is supported in part by a Bronx Community Artist Grant
awarded by Spaceworks. The Spaceworks Bronx Community Artist Grant
program is made possible through support from The New York Community Trust.
Additional support for the project was provided by
BxArts Factory and The Bronx Library Center.

SPACEWORKS

For all

the Women

who are certain   they are   the most powerful

kind of

Magic

The Details

Who:
A group of women of various ages, experiences and identifiers who set down fear to carry their pens and pull at the holy roar caught in feet, hands, heart and head.

What:
Participated in a workshop series titled "Robleswrites Productions Presents: Mujeres, The Magic, The Movement and The Muse". The workshops were led by Peggy Robles-Alvarado and guest facilitators Manuela Arciniegas (Palo Practicioner), Shihan Candy Warixi Soto (Taino Elder) and Jacqueline Odusinya Martin (Lukumi Priestess). We shared knowledge of traditional practices used for clearing or shifting energy and accessed creative muses women naturally carry within them by coaxing memories, soothing what ails, and restoring connections between body and spirit. The result: the *Magic* found in this collection.

Where:
The Bronx Library Center

Why:
because women centered workshops are necessary / because our bodies hold narratives / because we are more than just the fall / because we are taught to embrace everyone but ourselves / because we are not always a fist / because there is an intimate calligraphy etched in our spines / because we welcome the unapologetic and refuse to regret it / because we pulled throb and pulse from our throat chakras / because we are learning to quench the thirst of touch / because we are learning to pull Joy from unpolished stones charged under the full moon / because we are learning the language of our bodies.

When: October 2016

Gratitude

For the Spaceworks Bronx Community Artist Grant program and Raul Rivera who are certain The Bronx is and will forever be art.

For every woman who trusted me enough to dedicate Saturdays in October to a fearless dose of self-care, healing and artistic expression. Thank you, Modupe, Gracias - You are *Magic* and muse.

For Manuela Arciniegas who taught us how to appreciate each moment living from red to white sun, emulating our individual moyo with flare as we dance to the mambos we wrote for ourselves. Nsala malekum...

For Shihan Candy Warixi Soto who taught us how to soothe the forgotten chakra of breath with tabanuco and stones. Han Han katú!

For Jacqueline Odusinya Martin who taught us we were born sacred, selected our own Ori and must preserve it in order to fulfill our destinies. Bendición.

For Jean Harripersaud and Michael Alvarez of The Bronx Library Center and Yolanda Rodriguez from BxArts Factory for your support in securing a venue for the muses to write wild and free.

For Nia Andino who tugged at spirit and flesh to create the cover art that embodies the beauty and agony of all we released and created during our sessions together. You are third eye and vertabrae. Thank you for holding space and time.

For the eyes and heart of Yoseli Castillo Fuertes and Janel Cloyd.

For my family Jorge, Shanice, Indio, Nauel, Dyani, and Kiko for being the push. *#magicmakingisnotforpendejas*

For spirit that infuses the feet, legs, torso, arms, hands, breathe, eyes and head of women with stories to tell.

Contents

Aurora J. "AJ" De Peña

Joy I Sea

Aurora J. "AJ" De Peña

My Joy smells like salt
spread across the floor
curando the deep cuts under my feet

My Joy looks like smiling faces
vast embraces
saludándome back

My Joy tastes like vinagre blanco
sprinkled on the onions
I simmer on my pan

My Joy touches my skin softly
and rushes all at once
in an infinite hug of Paz

My Joy is tronadora like me
with each roaring call
making me powerful

Marionette
Aurora J. "AJ" De Peña

Spine
       Wings
             Back
                  Lungs
       Rib cage

The charge from her fingers

                  Transferred
          The battery
      Full
          Bending
Resting
       Jolting a smile
             Release
Deep breath

My back enjoys touch
             Revived
Like I could

Fly

When My Name No Longer Be Dawn
Aurora J. "AJ" De Peña

As I approach the white sun
and the low lights begin to pool in my eyes
I'd leave with no regrets
knowing I transformed lives
        with a simple hug
nothing left unsaid-
'I'm sorry'
and 'Thank you'
Dropped seeds in potted hearts
        Joy
        Harmony
        Peace
        Hope
to grow in simple pleasures
of sometimes being in pure silence
or extremely loud;
        In *complete* company with yourself
at times, in absolute surrender
to fuckery

My Right Hand Is Me
Aurora J. "AJ" De Peña

Fist enclosed
Ready
       fight
       tense
       angry
       upset
       tight

Most days
I keep my hand curled up
punching through life
exhausted white knuckles
painful sweaty palm

Today I release
open my hand
receive
one finger at a time
I wear each ring

     release

         healing

                  power

         strength

    love

Dual Gift

Aurora J. "AJ" De Peña

My hands create
what no one can destroy
This much I know to be truth
Yet I often fall victim to the lie
reflected in my mirror

My affirmations come up short
I don't trust the power
harvested within my hands
I hold back
drop the pen

In its beautiful words
flow my strength
Intangible things
that no one perceives
I can do

I initiate my own pain and my own healing
I am the owner of that gift
and it radiates to the page
from my connected joints
to the most broken parts of me

Citrine

Aurora J. "AJ" De Peña

clear as mid-afternoon
sparks of amber
salt
caramel tones
hard body
soft touch
my eyes see
both sides of you
like a human
I can trust
intricate details
of beauty
simplicity
like summer
like beach
where my soul feels at ease
skipping rocks in the sea
you give me a sense of peace
reminding me that even as
seasons change
I still carry the sun
like summer
like beach
In the tones of my own skin
and I am whole

Body Armor
Aurora J. "AJ" De Peña

arms wrap to protect
I embrace human flesh
on loving chest
nurture the worries away
like a mother's breast milk
body of a warrior
soul of a savior
transmitting warmth
with fire in my gut
keeps it alive with the blowing
air of my lungs
breaking down barriers
through a protective coat
I am strong
within
yet gentle
bending and molding
malleable and squeezable
dodging *punzadas* on the left
          and *latigazos* on the right
I thrive
to *cuidar* what's mine
radiating life
same as giving it
giving of me to you

Aurora's Mambo
Aurora J. "AJ" De Peña

Aurora de mi amanecer
Bella como las flores
Baila, brinca y goza
deja ya to' los dolores

Aurorita de mi cielo
Vámonos pa' la calle
A comelnos un yaniqueque
Pa' que te me ponga fuerte

Aurora de mi amor
mira que tu eres strong
No amanesca por ahi
jugando con Colibri

Aurorita preciosa
Baila, brinca y goza
Suelta ya to'ese duelo
Sea ese tu único anhelo

Oh Aurora
Oh my Dawn
Ay Aurora
Ay Amor

Tina B. Marie

You Smell Of Home
Tina B. Marie

> Pillows filled with scent of you
> laying in the embrace of ghosts
> following passerby after
> gut punch memory
> your phantom jolts me out of every day
> out of monotony and into you and me
> intertwined and apart like mutiny
> they send you to me
> on street corner collisions
> in boroughs not our own
> I breathe you in like lost promise
> inhaling halo heads of spirits crowned
> at same moment and spread like confetti
> to fated finding and fragrance to guide
> you smell like home
> every time
> every galaxy
> every alternate route
> we uttered a spell break
> universal mistake yet none such
> stuffed with hesitance at forward mobility
> holding to the fading wafting whiff of
> your meant to be warmth
> waiting for the love
> Oshun surely has in store
> meant leave me but expected
> you to hold on for more
> time bidding
> tongue biting
> never briding
> what's meant to be
> will not hide in shadows
> hurt in light or
> be a lost scent over night

You May

Tina B. Marie

Do bible writers breathe
the tales they weave
I can formulate and gesticulate
advise and cajole
Slide into the comfort
of a false role
predetermine and assist
but cannot head to heart
insist they desist
cannot follow
what mind says to hand
in constant silent battle
with what should
and could and is
the Plan
living a path
to be written
will this road breed folklore
lesson or reason to listen
you are psalms worming in
you are epitaphs
on the tombstone of departure
maps for unearthed souls
bathing in your
eternal internal scripture

The Weightlessness
Tina B. Marie

Tree trunk
less glorious
having marveled
at pajón
from above
how else can we catch ripened fruit

What bird
loves dirt
under toe
when its
tasted sky
under feather
save for lacking nourishment of earth

Mirth thief
baring teeth
dripping with
"once was"
"could have"
the future is grounded, stable

Cast away
discard unworthy
reborn this
wingless form
to lust
lost flight
were the winds simply too heavy for your light

¿Quién soy sin mi muleta?
Tina B. Marie

If you were not your anxiety
who would you be?

llámame madre de Kairi
hija de la Luna
que entiende el León

aquella que cura sin saber como
de las manos cubiertas en sangre

If you were not your anxiety
who would you be?

Calliope
Ella de la boca cerrada
que sola grita páginas

Ella que vive con un corazón rompido
pero ama doble con los pedazos

Si no fueras su ansiedad
¿Quién serías?

Everything.

Milagro

Tina B. Marie

Leoncio says he sees you
perched on the steps
watching him play
in Luz's daycare

I wonder if you rest there
watching one half
of your twins
we all
visit here most often

Your sons have needed you
every second since your departure
they still disagree
over who belonged at your side
in the ambulance

You matriarch
puzzle center
this picture makes no sense
without you
Holidays have lost their magic
my father the light in his eyes

Your husband is dying now
I cannot bring myself to his bedside
He must have hurt you so much
that must be why your heart
gave so young

They say it was your weight
but what would your soul do
living in an earthly body
too small to contain its glory

I still remember your simple meals
scrambled eggs
white rice
ketchup
I rarely ate back then
your love filled me
with even those small bites

Your guidance is felt
what can I do for you
when all you carry
when all you love
are too heavy
to move toward white sun

7 children
17 grandchildren
5 great grandchildren

You must be so busy
so unlived
so unfinished
Are you waiting for Porfirio?
Will you ask him if being
a mujeriego
was worth
our loss
?

Foliage Lineage
Tina B. Marie

For every one of my faltering steps
I see my children have taken
two assured strident footfalls
For every struggle that strangled
stifled & engulfed me
I witness leaps of forward faith from them

I failed to change my world entirely off words
instead I have shaped it by the action
of souls rebirthed
Let them shift the gravity & set right
taking my musings & creating masterpieces
Letting ideas come to physical fruition
at their miraculous hands

From white sun to zenith
I see them upon my shoulders
Shoulders sore from labor
head heavy with knowing
bloodied hands from bringing forth
& assisting in the departure of life
I have been a portal

Breasts shifted to map
green routes to areola
all passions combining
lactating personal nirvana
The eyes of my same souls
see not my toil
but gather in the warmth
of my content continent

The path of my life
littered with fruit
watered by determination
abundant enough so that
generations after will be sustained
I've planted only two seeds
but proliferated a forest
I the river
Matriarch
smile & flow
Descending

Jossie Ortiz

Puño
Jossie Ortiz

I am a Fist. Clenching. Unknown.
Searching. Needing reassurance.
A Fist. Subservient to energy.
To unknown answers. Fist. Closed.
Too tight for touching. Too tight
for breathing. Envying those that
do not dwell in the past. That will not
dwell for past lives. That see beauty
in me. Within me. Within my shadows.
Beauty that I cannot always release.
Illness carved into me. Leaving
behind uncertainty. Creating loneliness.
I am not always a clenched fist.
Not always a fist clenched.
There are days when my petals open.
Days that I unclench my fist
to you. Remember if I do
it is because I've welcomed
loving you.

How Is It We Bend Yet Never Break?
Jossie Ortiz

The spine
curved
and
shaped
by
knotted
roots
&
bark
from
thunder
storms
&
crying
heaven

all in memory
all in formation

The spine
remembers
wings
that
glided
into
spaces
unreachable
by
man
by
birds
by
us

This
is
why

Before time
we reached into existence
We were organisms of the moon

We stretched into cosmos
We were dream creators

when
we
are
born
we
start
to
fear
the
highest
peak

It
reminds
us
of
scissors
that
shredded
feathers

I Speak a Language of Fragrance
Jossie Ortiz

Closed eyes
Cleansing dirty lungs

inhale self- doubt
exhale spice
exhale smudged mints

                    musk

                        captured

                in
                            between

                                    my

                    teeth

I speak a language of fragrance

each herb pressed under my feet
before bed

its scent roaming the hallways
free from walls / cages / phobias

a fragrance,

            light as your last breath

                    right before death stretched out
                    her hands

Slumber,
Jossie Ortiz

You visit often the dark corners of my subconscious. Offering gifts of deep exhales in your serenity. The tingles of your trace felt on the tip of my neck. There, between the head and lump on my back. Tangible markings on the surface of my skin, left behind from your kisses. Birth marks of past and future lives, twenty two remembrances of when I ran barefoot through wet vivid soil; the amount of passages from her womb, even if prematurely.

At times I still fear the flashbacks of the trauma in our blood line. The pain our flesh has endured from branches that stretched from our very own planted trees. The trauma of brokenness inherited into unheard screams and illegal trespasses into virgin lands. Days that still drain me even when I cleanse myself through coffee strainers by the stove and I wish at times for your company when bones start to crackle and my legs become heavy.

Just as I find myself photographing into my sub-consciousness the waves of the sky. The movements of birds. Listening for the crow's warrior cries. My heart preparing herself when hearing just one song. Praying that in the distance there are two in flight. Fidgety in forgiving my own survivors remorse.

Yet, my daughter has become my reminder in the mornings of the preciousness, in rebirth, and pain. I find myself writing letters on patchouli petals and parchment paper. Letters compelling my daughter to never be ashamed of the coils in her hair, her size, nor the shape of her hips. To be gentle to herself, to her womanhood. To not bite her lips when angry and to stay away from lighters attached to toxins. A legacy of words that Mami forgot to tell me.

I find myself needing to hide away into the earth's unhealed wounds.
The heaviness of thoughts,
"Am I good enough?"

The anxiousness of keeping my hands in my pocket, trying not to bite my nails, remembering to look at everyone in the eyes and smile.
"Why am I not happy enough?".

Needing to drown hand-me- downs of ragged skin and lies that still flow through our lineage. This chain of wretchedness, may it rust with each exhale of breath.

Slumber, may it wrap me up in infinite peace. May I be allowed the adequate amount of time to leave memories of smiles. For I know life has taught me well, regardless of the fears flushing through my eyes. I pray to take with me all those aches. May they all be consumed in the never ending sea.

Yours Truly,

Jossie Ortiz

Calligraphy
Jossie Ortiz

I am in the hues that whisper drum beats into starving mouths
                    Electromagnetic waves
pushing hairs to stand on end

Hypnotic lengths of visions
            as the curtains are
                        pulled by their
                            hinges

Revealing
        mouth

Vibrant in clover
            molasses
                &
            bee stings

Walls stripped down to the core
all of its syrupy delusions
peeled off clean
My intimate calligraphy strokes
the sand before the tsunami
The thunder before boisterous storms

                                        Exhuming
                                        lungs
                                        with
                                        herbs
                                        and
                                        smoke

            Thickening ideologies on tongues of fire
                    with bitter sweet residue
                            of pain
            of euphonious songs crocheted with survival
                Exchanging breath through pulping lips
        Exchanged through touch and colors still unbirthed into existence

26

Café con leche
Jossie Ortiz

Through jittered fingers
molasses of earth and grains
rinsed through smirks
&
bitter enchantments
Tranquilizing those unsettling things
those unexplained premonitions
that crash you from existence

Summer heat
A warmth that connects your nervous
system to your soul
&
spirit

Deep inside the belly
A lava of Caribbean sand
drenches your veins down to the ends of
your feet

Feeds you empathy to the morning sun
Spilling into your memories of wuelita's rich
exuberance

Colador
digesting into you a fraction of elation
and tonics
with its white cotton

Nia Andino

Two Trainings, Same Body
Nia Andino

My body started its greatest lesson at the saltmouth of Megan's Bay
where I grasped floating above my grandfather's palms
a rite of passage
for Yankee bodies to become versed in home cures
with each swallow of brine
I am no stranger here
the sand on my stomach knows me
dug into me
under bright orange poly
atop a deepening sun
I thought there is no leaving here
when I gave the ocean my back
the waves
my core

But

at the Queens YMCA
swim class pinned me to its belly unnoticed
contained water pushed 400 year inherited memories
on a 9 year old back
lungs cursed me in chlorine
on how not to drown
and the heart administered tolls
for what I let fill me

the crawling started
as an education on how to save myself
or lest become repeated histories
of sunken survivors
buttoned to the bottom of blue floors

The Tutelage of My Core
Nia Andino

Now I've come to understand
a pained stomach is a talk with
my great- grandmother
Her twisted intestines
     transformed
        to
           unraveled
             phone
           cords
              in me

We are always connected
With every pang she reminds me of what
happens when I fail to trust my gut

See I was a colicky baby
lungs shrill enough to set my father a tumbled
pawn on an outside bench for weeks
It is how I learned power gnaws at you from
the inside first if you don't let it out

Early on, my mother pressed cotton and penny
        where/they/severed/us
         to remodel our breach into Hawaiian slit pretty
        but my navel fought
        to dip
        wide and cavernous

This is how my body taught me not to be so accepting
even when love carries familiar in its hands

31

Of Footsteps In Shadows
Nia Andino

They say you walked in with me
heck, all the women up my line

veiled face
same gap
ojos de almendra
You,
who whisper dust in our eyes and say it's for clarity
dar la luz to bodies ravaged with too much sweetness
for so much voice

Then you remove things...
toes
limbs
breasts
sight
to lessen our weight
and place fright in a fate reborn from yours
so we pray in your war room
tending the pain pitted in your stomach that blooms
You watch our bodies swaying
arms like sprinklers
trying to leak your sorrows into floor dances
with rum
and spillage
cause there is always spillage

We bargain your ears with flores
leave reflections of you in the river
follow you follow us to the edge
where I attempt to build you a proper heaven
with purple willows to hang your scars
and dried fruit to soak up your weeping

I know you will find us again
tucked in the wind like sillage and saltwater

I hope this time you find someone to slip into
who measures all of this life with love
and carries lessons like rising bread

Mouth of A Marinera
Nia Andino

here,
a bed of saltines
okra + cornmeal
gandules seated
on the hollow of emptying coconuts
a churn of Danish butter

pa'lla,
brush fires and cinders spread
upon a tongue of fattened memories
adding this taste of earth when my eyelids shutter
until the body revives itself
every morning at 3am

soy marinera
dragging barnacles and heat on a perfumed and shipwrecked mouth
pulling scabs from seawater

for each new day
I break fasts
and masticate on magas + honey
coercing distended belly to clear it's air of salt and suffering
from the remnants of yesterday's war

Medicine for Medusa
Nia Andino

What served as our summer home
is the place where my mother grew legs
the place where I most stretched mine

per usual
July gave us her late heat
settled it around my bitten and pretzeled limbs
demanding relief from a cool floor

I remember the day
when that amber porcupine emerged from the folds of my packed things
boar bristled brush lengthening to the darkest brown
strands unbending after 5 days of holding

"You didn't know I knew how to do hair, did you?"

my grandfather asked me through tender partings
shadowshaping me a Medusa
recycling memories through fingers
extending the childhood of my mother

I had not known men to care for heads
only the protecting of bodies

my eyes fixated on the indoor hammock
and the sliding glass door revealing the dark halo
hugging my great uncle's head
he walked in
as if born on stilts
and bent down to lend my face his smile
these 2 brothers are now deep in my head
conferring over wounds of an itchy scalp

then, I am led by my uncle's hand
and his traveling breath
colored in rum
to the cabinet of bushes and medicine living in the backyard
he breaks the plant with teeth

giving me some of its jelly
applies the rest to my head
over a song that is stuck in his

"This is for your scars. For all types of them," he says

then returns me to my grandfather
with a hand full of healing
and a refreshed head

Tamara G. Saliva

The Casing
Tamara G. Saliva

There is scripture here
between collar bone and belly pouch
    Motherhood
drafted in stretched skin
     over curves
I have decorated in scars
the casing of my spirit
      in an attempt to remove the blemish of
my reflection
I am still learning to accept what is in my vision
Still learning how to love what was once
         damaged
Still learning how to be gentle with myself
     No longer dissecting
the flesh that houses my soul

My Joy

Tamara G. Saliva

Often his eyes remind me of his father

His nose

       arrow shaped pointed down

His smiles and smirks are cut from him

His face-

His face is exactly like mine

I look forward to greeting him when I walk through the door

although he is sweaty and smells like a dirty boy

I tend to remind him of needing a shower for a belly full of laughs

My Joy

I forget how I've earned his love

      I don't think he should love me the way he does

        I'm lucky

Sometimes I sit with myself-

remind myself

I deserve this joy

     I deserve his love

        I deserve his love

          I deserve his love

I deserve to be loved by my son

Grandmother I Am Coming To Know
Tamara G. Saliva

I can hear you in regressive stumbling,
tangled between realms.
The sound of your confusion awakens me.
Your backward days and delayed development
weigh heavy on the strings of my fate.

Come,
Grandmother I never knew,
follow the flickering light in the center
of my palms.
Walk with me.
I have called to the four winds
for guidance on this journey.

They have whispered:
She does not know what she seeks.
You must take her to the fountain of clarification.
Educate her in ritual and prayer.
Lay the foundation for her position.
Your discipline is the bases of her refinement.
Should she choose to accept it,
there is a new destiny awaiting
her on the other side of your prayers.

Come,
Grandmother,
Mother of my Father,
follow the moisture lines of hope. They will
lead you to the droplets of light and progress.
Sit with me.
Grandmother I am coming to know,
Set your sight on this fountain; it is for the
clarity of your message by way of my lips.
Accept this flame. Take it into your spirit
so that you may elevate into enlightenment.

Grandmother,
soul of my familial commission,
I open my ears to the sound of your guidance.
My heart and soul open for the glitter of your magic,
open for the teachings of your witching.
I wish to commune with you through cigar smoke,
cups of coffee and the blowing of fire water.
Grandmother I am coming to know,
the remaining days of this life cycle
will now be layered in your guidance.

        Padre nuestro.....

Yadhira Gonzalez-Taylor Esq.

Sweet Soft Quick Sand*
Yadhira Gonzalez-Taylor, Esq.

Mountains of quick sand

with pink colored striations

Marked by time and weight

Valleys of flesh nestled in hills

The pink colored scars from a thousand tiger paws

Once fertile, now barren

A soft resting place

For my lover's delight

His head and his eyes

his gratefulness shows

To be laying in sweet

soft

quicksand

Inspired by Comrade Bliss Ain't playing by Josefina Baez (2008)

Invisible Ink
Yadhira Gonzalez-Taylor, Esq.

Tattooed on the canvas of my spirit are
the memories of your love.
Outlined in blood and tears,
inked with whips and chains
as I walk among the living.

Tattooed on the cardboard box of your shame are
the memories of your hate.
Outlined in insanity, anxiety, and dread.
Inked in shallow breaths and dark thoughts
as the memory of your ashy grave travels down the Hudson River.

Tattooed in the story of my life
are the people, places, and things you never knew.
Outlined in wholesome treasures made of miracles and curly tresses
inked in spaces filled with love
as the dreary memory of yesterday fades.

Tattooed in the cosmos of my tomorrows
and the tomorrows of their tomorrows
is the family you will never know.
Outlined in sunny mornings where all is a glow
inked in notes of love perfumed in care and comfort
as if you never existed.

I Am A Goddess, I Am Here To Be Loved
Yadhira Gonzalez-Taylor, Esq.

I came into the world crowned by a ring of fire
The universe whispered: **You are a Goddess, You are here to be loved**

I left the safety of my mother and I heard the air say:
The breeze of the ocean will whisper I love you
The sand will kiss your feet
The laughter of children will be your jester
Their cries will be your oracle

I responded while I still knew:
I am a goddess and I am here to be loved
I will be lulled to sleep by singing tree frogs
My hair will be brushed by the humidity of a thousand Cimarrones
Rainforest's morning dew will always kiss my forehead and make
me seem aglow

The clouds will sing blue skies when I am happy
and turn grey when I am not
They will thunder with my anger
and rain to cleanse the ground

Rose petals will line the streets of my dirty gritty city
I'll step upon them, releasing their perfume
Cooling feathers will flutter near me on hot summer days
Angels, doves, and canaries will sing as I walk along

The stars and moon will always watch me
To remind me when I go astray
They will sprawl the message out on lit skies
I am a goddess, and here today and always, simply to be loved

I Create With My Hands What Can't be Destroyed
Yadhira Gonzalez-Taylor, Esq.

Life, love, tenderness, support, and memories
Days painted on molecules of dust
Quiet mornings hidden in green
Communing with jade, dumb cane, succulents and philodendrons

Memories, recorded in stereo through the whispers of leaves
Memories, etched in water drops and mist
Memories, preserved in variegation and thankfulness for nurture

Life, love, tenderness, support, and memories
Days recorded on early morning sun beams
Quiet mornings hidden in music notes from medieval strings
Communing with pothos, mal padre, money tree, and rubber plant

Memories, recorded in grounded eggshells
Memories, etched in coffee grinds and filters
Memories, preserved in the feedings and aeration of hatchling
red wigglers

Life, love, tenderness, support, and memories
Days recorded in the castings of their droppings
Quiet mornings hidden in the harvesting of food
Communing with soil, sand, peat moss, and perlite

Memories, recorded in conversations with my daughters
Memories, etched in examples of the properties of aloe
Memories, preserved in the quietude of love

Cindy Peralta

Purify Your Sound
Cindy Peralta

My thoughts
     are filthy.

        They've been dragged
     through insecurity and depression.

               Sullied by
          anxiety and self-deprecation,

and I can't seem to get the **stain**
of **regret** and **guilt** out of the fabric of my spirit.

     Flushing them out with ancient magic
        and holy water.
        Healing
     the scar tissues of abuse
    bonded into the creases of my Ori
       without drowning.

  Thought I'd die

       if I ever had to live without.

Only realizing their limitations,
        keep me dirty

and
   I'm
     dying
       to
         get clean.

If A Rose Were Any Other Name
Cindy Peralta

I speak a language of fragrance.
A slight mixture of
lavender, gardenia, roses,
honey and manure.

Easy for it to get lost in translation.
My prickly thorns
can cut down the thickest of skins.

Honey coated rainfalls
cleanse my palate
allowing its true nature
to waft into the noses
of those cursing my tongue

Who knew love could be so bittersweet?

How much blood will you shed
when pricked for those who you love,
before realizing, there are flowers
just as beautiful
that don't cause so much pain?

When I Approach The White Sun
Cindy Peralta

When I approach the white sun,
      I want to leave joy in my wake.

I want the world to finally see me!

That I laughed,
     smiled,
          lived,
               loved,
                    cried,
                         almost died
                              then did die

               and came back to life.

       Not comparing myself to Jesus
                             but
                                 more like the ocean
                                  with its
                                  ebb & flow,
                     revealing outgrown shells left by
                       hermit crabs.
                That is what I shall leave.
            Treasures of homes for those in need,
         trinkets for beach combers to pick up
and put in their pocket.
Taking pieces of my magic.
             Knowing that each time they look at me,
                 they smile.
                         That source of a moment in
               time
           that they were one with me.

To pass on to my sons,
   recipe of wave making that
return us to our beginnings,

  as they age
    crashing away from the sun as it sets.
      Not understanding
       true tranquility,
        true peace they will seek.
          Until they
       swim
      further out from shore,

     treading water in the unknown,

    being in the now,

   a victim of the current,

  with their faces towards the sun,

  absorbing the warmth of pure heaven,

   finally being one...

 with me

Melissa "Emalia" Medina

The Descent

Melissa "Emalia" Medina

As I approach the white sun I will feel at ease

descending

calmly

floating between flesh and spirit

as if I've done so

one thousand

times

before

Upon my descent I will leave sound waves

vibrating at the level of all that is

&

all that will ever be

Of moments blessed

portals opened

Where conga drums

will guide

The rest of my bloodline

home

Black Kyanite
Melissa "Emalia" Medina

Your vibrations are ancient

Invoking visions of past lives

Your arrow head piercing right into my self-worth

My thoughts

stretch towards all the points

I thank fire, air, water and earth

I praise the divinity

Knees bent on cold ground

I swallow you whole

Bathe in your flow

Behold,

you are just 1 of 2 stones to stand alone

Deflecting all that comes to me in

VENOM

and placing it before me as sacred

MOSS

I place you between me and the Heavens

A pathway home

Blessed be

my mighty stone

The Calligraphy Of My Existence
Melissa "Emalia" Medina

So restless was I to be done with it all

The Heavens wanted me home

Lovingly stitched

Each blood clot formed

Kissed

by every dark horse

of my lineage

Burdens placed on my skin

Cursed

Heart-synced

with the un-forgiven

and

within my lungs

every breath

waited

to breathe

once again

So restless was I to be done with it all

The Heavens wanted me home

Janel Cloyd

Mapping The Atlas of a Woman's Spine
Janel Cloyd

Place your pregnant thumbs on the base of your spine.
Breathe.
Listen
                    to the messages planted there from your birth.
Breathe
Inhale
                    the possibilities resting beneath your skin.

Breathe
Exhale
                    the stardust housed in your throat.

Breathe

Women,
Use your female hands.
Rub palms to skin.
Explore the geography of your body.
Reveal the shimmer of a moon's daughter.

Women,
Memorize each rung of the ladder residing in your back.
Always have remembrance of your underpinning.
Cervical
Thoracic
Lumbar
Sacral
Coccyx

Women,
We bend but, we never break.
33 bones within the lining of your vertebrae
conspire to stretch
You are taller than any obstacle.

Women,
We must claim ownership
of our spines.
There will always be
someone trying to climb
the stairway of our backbone.

I Am Not Always A Fist
Janel Cloyd

I am Not Always a Fist.
Sometimes.
I am.
Outstretched.
Hand.
Inviting you
Into the river
of my body.
Come here.
Sing into my neck.
Lay your hands.
on my throat.
Finger by finger.
Invite me to gargle
and yodel our love song.
Note by note.
Together
We will cast.
Our song into the wind.
Our hearts.
Will scatter like
Fallen.
Leaves.
As they make
decisions to die
and become born
again.

Flora Montes

My Heart
Flora Montes

My heart lives
in an abyss of complacency.
In a world where impressions
are meant to last a lifetime.
Forgiveness reigns truth.

As my heart searches
for redemption
in the solemn pink
of your saintly eyes.
Where sanity suffers
from too much analysis,
as the intrinsic symphony
at first soft and sweet,
then loud and clear,
screams for absolution.

A mere rippling of gentle sounds
delicately woven in etched stone
causing melodies, sways
danced upon calloused feet.

Longing to enter your palace of
dreams, draped in jewels and gold.
Where angels play sweet
melodies in beautiful hues.
Awakened from deep slumber,
as harmonic notes
entwine with the ocean,
becoming one
in a trance with an epiphany.

Sydney Valerio

Alegría
Sydney Valerio

As I approach the white sun
I want to leave my zeal for life
my abilities to move forward and
succeed although I have faced strife
I will not need to navigate
so many different locations
because when I enter the white sun
I will be greeted by familiar faces

Mamá Anta
will tell how much
Mami was like me
as a kid

Tío Tono
will hug me
tightly till I say
¨Tío, I need to breathe!¨
as he brings me to
the middle of the circle
so I can imitate his dance moves
to the merengue beats

Our movement together
will happen effortlessly
we've done this many times before
and my spirit will be able to rest
and be at peace
while surrounded by a feast
commemorating the day I pass
just like the day
I was born
full of thanksgiving

Whisperings
Sydney Valerio

The whispering souls in my lineage
traveling many lands and across seas
have not left any signs of torment
that they have not dealt with privately
Each member of my large family
when presented with choice of
self care or of preserving family
has kept the tug of war within them
the way anyone would who doesn't
have firm ground under their feet

Their relocation from Santiago
to the countryside of Montecristi
during a dictatorship and
several U.S. occupying armies
most likely created torment in the family
that should still be felt by me
Stories are not discussed at family gatherings
only some times Tio Julio pulls me aside to confide in me
'Yo tenía que reportar los que faltaron cada día
para trabajar la finca pero no lo hacia
porque luego desaparecían'
His account of that era emphasizing
the power of words I hold dearly

I hear other whisperings at times rustling through the breeze,
I actually see them written amongst the trees,
as I hike through Bronx woods
and feel the connection between the earth and me.
I feel the whisperings at times,
the air cups my ear and tells me
I have been at this river or beach before

when I visit el Morro.
The ocean's waves collide and
their foaming bubbles greet my feet,
I do not fear being swallowed up,
I actually go in too deep.
I climb down hills, to access the 'raw' beach,
place my bare feet over volcanic rocks
whose smooth surfaces are quite hot.
I pick one up and notice
the seashell imprint
made centuries ago like
whisperings imprinted in my soul.

They are there, not stuck, but pushing me
to grow, to listen, to love, to heal and to let go.
Can these whisperings control my growth
in a capitalist society that measures
my success based on what I own?
Mami says don't take the seashell with me
or I'll never have a love of my own.
I continue collecting
the rocks and the seashells
to take back to New York.
Satisfied with the idea
of not holding on to anything:
not a home, not a car,
not a man, not his heart,
not his soul.

Clave

Sydney Valerio

huhhh huhhh huhhh
huhhh huhhh
huhhh huhhh huhhh huhhh huhhh
huhhh huhhh huhhh
huhhh huhhh
huhhh
huhhh
huhhh
huhhh
huhhh
huhhh huhhh huhhh
huhhh huhhh
huhhh
huhhh
huhhh
huhhh huhhh
huhhh huhhh
huhhh huhhh huhhh
(insert your name)
remember to
b r e a t h e
love
heal
s p e a k
write
your story
huhhh huhhh huhhh
huhhh huhhh
b r e a t h e

Puños y Trompones
Sydney Valerio

I am not always a fist full of
tightly sealed sticky
pink wrapped
Duble Bubles
my aunt brought me
from Castañuelas
chicles that lose their flavor
after five chews

yes, I counted how
ah one
ah two
ah three
ah four
ah five
yes, 'ah five' chews later

s t r e t c h e d   g u m

hardened now by the cold air
once softened by the humidity found in
el colmado del campo
THERE
they were as soft as the
wrinkled nuez moscada skin of mi tia's puño
HERE
this chicle is as hard as un TROMPÓN

pink crown adorned paper wrapper
tightly pressing on its contents
so as to contain
its American dream full power

an overly sugary taste
combined with a
non-producing bubbling thrust
after all it is a
fist full of American gum SOLD in el campo
brought *BACK* to The States five chews later you can see
that cycle of puños y trompones are really not me.

I am not always a fist full of

d   i   s   p   l   a   c   e   m   e   n   t

sometimes I am the puño de ajo que llega
"a buen tiempo" you place me into el pilón
mash me into the mix of
plátanos fritos   y   chicharrón
and my substance
will try to help you not forget
how to form
el mofongo and
how it too
is a mixed
fist one full
de un trompón de raíces
de e l a s t i c i t y
de sabor
de caña sweetness y
"buen provecho"

71

Jama Clark

Sweet Light
Jama Clark

Since I was a child, my favorite time of morning
has always been dawn

That time of day when the sky is no longer
completely dark, but the sun hasn't quite risen

Referred to by photographers as the sweet light
Either optimism or despair grows in those few minutes

The time where the delectable taste of hope or
the sour sting of a hangover presents itself

It is a time of day that represents choice or consequence

Time stood still for me the day you left
The power of choice, that sweet light was stolen

I could tell by all of the tools you left me
that you wanted to help me make better choices

Did you make it safely?

You never called.

I made you a care package just in case you need it
Some tools and comforts to help on your journey:

A white candle to light the path
Dunkin Donuts coffee (no cream, no sugar)
Snapple Ice Tea
Cigar
A Blue pouch filled with items that represent gratitude
A White pouch filled with items that represent hope
A Red pouch filled with items that represent power
A purple pouch filled with items that represent empathy
A small jar of honey
A brown paper bag with nine pennies inside (You should always have
some money)
Another with candies inside
Some white rum
Some cool water
Your Issi Miyaki cologne

74

If you need anything else you can best reach me
at my favorite time of morning

That time of day when the sky is no longer
completely dark, but the sun hasn't quite risen

You can catch me in the sweet light

Peggy Robles-Alvarado

Nonet for Mujeres de Monte
Peggy Robles-Alvarado

Stand, stretch limbs from red sun to zenith.
Tap at the moyo in your chest.
There is no maña like yours!
Sing mambos to yourself-
you are ancient prayer,
palo santo,
bendita
eres
tú.

Bop For Our Bodies or
How Mother Can Be In(art)iculate
Peggy Robles-Alvarado

I was told soothing is for toddlers wrapped around our legs, the scowl
of sciatica second to hide and seek, no time for stretching between songs
& silly faces. Rubbing is for bellies we fill even when ours rumble empty; we
chew on sacrifice & learn to love its taste. Hold is for spaces given to the
ones we call love, besides it is silly to try & hug yourself
& Mami said crying is for the weak.

It is dangerous to forget how we hurt

We grow deaf when the body speaks, tourniquets of tendon & muscle when
what we carry doesn't balance properly on hips or thighs or heart.
How wads of hair on a pillow are a pitchy chorus from wailing nerves, an
angry rash under the lip; graffiti from an overworked liver. The nightly
sparring match between grinding teeth & bleeding gums, the gotta
go, go go, don't waste no time, keep doing, & moving and brush it off.
Those tense shoulders welcome the title of strong woman even if it's
designed to vex us all into abandonment 'cause Tia said mothers can't be selfish.

It is dangerous to forget how we hurt

Maybe today we breathe rosemary oil into vertebrae that pinch / shift / swell, carry rose
quartz in front pockets reminding the pelvis it was weapon before holster, twirl yerba
buena around tongues until the mambo we wrote for ourselves drips down our chins.
Maybe today we press forgiveness to our chests, let it feed until perfection is gone
& we set down the pain others celebrate as selfless, reclaiming bodies as sanctuary/
isla / obra knowing we're not always a balled fist/an after- thought/ a muted roar.

We understand it is dangerous to forget how we hurt

Nonet For Mujeres and their Muses
Peggy Robles-Alvarado

Breathe, make time to listen to the howl;
the wild in you that calls to wind
and prays over clear water.
You have always been strength.
Superior one,
blessed creature-
run, live
Free.

A Lo' Sandra Cisneros or
For Angel Stephanie Who Thrives In Her Mother Tongue

Peggy Robles-Alvarado

You bring out the tíguera in me
The piernas inquietas, dedos en la boca in me
The Chicas del Can en pleno merengue in me
The dembow sonando en la jeepeta in me
The bachatéame pégaito in me
The fishnets and mini falda in me
The sucking on limoncillos and equimalitos in me
The ¡OFRÉSCOME! in me
The cúcara-mácara-títere fue in me
The no puedo estar quieta in me
The tengo que estar loca 'cause I
told your mom que se vaya pal carajo,
malagradecida in me
The your momma never liked me anyway,
so pa' la mierda in me
The don't care for talk from titiribundati in me
The chica mala in me
The mira mi chapa que vibra in me
The colín en la cadera in me
The tabaco y ron,
watermelon hookah encendía in me
The hoy se bebe in me
The Brugal de mallita in me
The ¡diantre que jumo! in me
The tú jeva tiene su son pero tú
quiere este tumbao in me
The privando en vaina in me
y ahora tú ta' quillao in me
The cójelo con take it easy in me
The ta' to, tamo claro in me
The dame luz in me
The necesito un desayuno de tres golpes
para matar esta resaca in me
The dame una Presidente bien fria in me
The me voy a poner caché bombita
y nos vamos a janguiar otra vez in me
'cause no me importa ni fu ni fa,
y yo no soy ninguna chapiadora
porque yo tengo mi propio cuarto
You bring out the montra in me
mujer sin escrúpulos, atrevida in me y
eso e' lo que te guta

Nonet For Lessons We Learned From Obatala's Daughter
Peggy Robles-Alvarado

Walk, head high on firm relaxed shoulders.
Honor Ori you chose at birth.
Cleanse it with milk and honey.
Press fontanelles firmly-
that's where life began!
Strengthen your crown,
for balance
love and
health.

Instructions For Pushing La Dolida Over The Kalunga Line
Peggy Robles-Alvarado

remove dust from her photograph / firmly press out creases / place in
frame / set frame over white tablecloth / light nine day candle fully aware
it will only burn for three / place clear glass full of cold water and candle
before frame / sit comfortably before frame / inhale / exhale / try to
say the name of the deceased nine times / say it at least three times /
watch bubbles emerge / dismiss logic / cease to explain away tightening
in your chest / do not call it goose bumps/inhale / exhale / fight urge to
grab sweater / accept the temperature has not changed / admit she has
arrived / inhale / do not clench jaw / uncross arms and legs / exhale / set
body to listen / fix ears to accept / fight urge to categorize this as crazy
/ define crazy / inhale / realize you are not crazy / exhale / recognize you
are present / understand she is in existence / reject notion that this is not
happening / inhale the smell of café negro / inhale the smell of jabón de
Maja / exhale / inhale the smell of rolos en la secadora /exhale /inhale
pages of an old bible / exhale / inhale / exhale/ inhale / watch flame
of the nine day candle that will burn for three dance with her shadow
/ exhale / cry if you must / discern your wailing from hers / eliminate
the immediate need to hold it all together / exhale agony she expected
to suffer for nine days but lasted three / exhale useless pride / exhale
impossibility of what is happening / inhale / exhale / watch the sun rise
over the flame / inhale / recite prayer for hardened souls / recite prayer
for tormented spirits / improvise prayer for the keepers of bitter women
/ sing the bolero she made anthem / continue to cry / inhale/ exhale /
sing a mambo for the Nkisi she hid from nosey neighbors in a wooden
cabinet / do not judge your voice / sing loud enough to stir her beyond
the white sun / inhale / exhale / allow your throat to propel her up and
over / forgive / forgive / inhale / forgive her / forgive yourself for being
just like her / exhale / repeat as needed / repeat as needed / repeat /
repeat / accept this as ritual / accept this / accept your feet are just like
hers but will walk different paths / accept you are the only one who can
open her road / accept you are the only one /
          / accept you
          / accept you are
          / accept you are the one
          / accept you are the only one who can

Bios

Aurora J. "AJ" De Peña

is a 35 year old hugger who loves to write; or a writer who loves to hug-depends who you ask. AJ has performed and featured at several open mics in New York including The Poets Settlement, Smokin' Word Open Mic Series, Sugarhill Beats, Soul House, Queens Lit Crawl, Tantalizing Angel Productions, and at The Nuyorican Poet's Cafe. As a member of the Full Circle Ensemble she has been featured in the Full Circle Ensemble's Stage Productions "Page to the Stage", "Misconceptions", "Misconceptions Too" and "Page 2: Standing in your Truth" at the National Black Theatre and was published in their anthology. For more information email her at aurdep@gmail.com.

Tina B. Marie

is a writer who after many life diversions is trying to find her way back to her foundation. She contributes to a weekly ezine at Sonder.NYC and will soon contribute to RoaringGold.com. She hopes to soon release a chapbook she has laid to the side for too long. She would love to participate in as many performances as possible, as she has only ever attended slams and open mics at the Nuyorican Poets Café and the Poets Passage in Puerto Rico. She hopes to have an official website one day, but for now can be found on most social networks under her handle @TinaBmarie.

Jossie Ortiz

is an Afro-Latinx queer poet and published author with ELKAT Productions who writes about raw topics in a story based format that cites personal situations dealing with social injustices, spirituality, mental illness, love and heartache. As an alumni of The Full Circle Ensemble, she is currently working on a compilation of poems for an upcoming chapbook and a One-Wo(man)-show. She is also in the process of editing a book titled "Dear Taueret- These are not our love poems", a collection of poems and personal essays depicting her first romantic encounter. Jossie has been featured at events produced by The Full Circle Ensemble at The National Black Theatre, ELKAT productions, JesPeachy, Gun Hill's Brewery: Performance & Pint and LatinosNYC at The Nuyorican Poets Cafe. She is always in gratitude for the support, teachings, and friendship of her peers, mentors and the community she is proud to be part of.

Nia Andino

is a visual artist and writer originally hailing from Queens, NY. Raised with the culture of Caribbean stories in her home, she is drawn to elements of visual and verbal expression that reflect her Latin/Caribbean roots, and the beauty and condition of the human soul. Nia holds a BFA in Interior Design from Parsons School of Design. Her art has been collected and shown at several galleries in New York, New Jersey and California including Pier 94, Aeon Logic, Abrazo Interno, Port Authority Terminal, Rio II, miLES, Center City, Rebelution Ink, The Brecht Forum and the Westin Bonaventure Hotel. Nia has also assisted in facilitating mural and art workshops taking place at the South Bronx Community High School and in the Lower East Side. In 2014, she participated in a live painting tribute to Frida Kahlo at the New York Botanical Gardens and created a painting for the art opening of the Nina Simone documentary The Amazing Nina Simone. Nia has been featured as a poet at the Nuyorican Poets Café and in Queens Lit Fest. Her art has been published in SmokeLong Quarterly and her writing has been published in Moko Magazine and The Abuela Stories Project anthology. Nia also designed the cover art for this anthology. You can view her work at www.andinostyles.com

Tamara G. Saliva

is a native Nuyorican born in Brooklyn N.Y. and raised on the borders of Harlem and Washington Heights. She is a self-published author of the book Blue Vein Pages, a self- taught artist, and jewelry maker. Her work has been published in the Hunter College Literary magazine, LETRAS and Sinister Wisdom 97: Out Latina Lesbians. She has been featured in numerous poetry showcases, including at The Nuyorican Poets Cafe. You can find her work at http://tamaragsaliva.wix.com/tamaragsaliva. You can also find her jewelry line at https://www.facebook.com/salivasimpletreasures/ www.etsy.com/shop/SimpleTreasureGifts.Instagram:@simpletreasuregifts She can be contacted at tamaragsaliva@aol.com

Yadhira Gonzalez-Taylor Esq.

is a public service Attorney who works with at risk youth in the New York City Department of Education. She came to writing and poetry through nightly story telling with her children. She is an avid indoor and outdoor gardener who loves to learn about the medicinal properties of herbs and spices and the benefits of gardening and self-sustainability.

Yadhira finds joy in cloning and propagating her houseplants, boasting a collection of over forty various species of houseplants. She is the author of two published illustrated children's books, Martina Finds a Shiny Coin and Martina and the Wondrous Waterfall. She was published in the anthology, Bronx Memoir Project from the Bronx Council of the Arts and contributes to her own blog Eggshell Gal Friday which can be found at egfriday. wordpress.com. Yadhira is a proud member of the Full Circle Ensemble Sunday Writing Circle and performed her spoken word with the Circle last fall in Harlem, NYC.

Cindy Peralta

is better known as Black Angel during times of poetic war and AnaCaona in times of peace. A guerrera salon- maker, superwoman mother to two superheroes in training and overall light bearer of badass awesomeness! A poet, spoken word performer, writer, monologist, actress and now published author, she is interested in pursuing the deepest crevices of her magic bag of talent to see what comes next. Her work can be found on youtube and various social media platforms including Facebook or follow her blog www.wordpress.blackangelthepoet.com. She's performed at The Nuyorican Poet's Cafe, Governors Island Poetry Festival, Dodge Poetry Festival, Eastern Correctional Facility, Riker's Island Correctional Facility and in the elusive train stations of the melting pot that is NYC. She can be reached via Facebook, by email at blackangelthepoet@gmail.com or morse code —...

Melissa "Emalia" Medina

was born in Rio Piedras, Puerto Rico and raised in Spanish Harlem during the 70s and 80s. She began journaling at a very young age and received a National Young Writer's Plaque in 6th grade. She is the author of Alpha Omega Poetry: Life Lessons and has featured at The Nuyorican Poet's Café, The National Black Theater and The Bronx Museum of The Arts. Emalia can be described as a low key poet with a lot of real-life personal experiences to share. Her words tend to hit deep, sometimes painful but always honest. She can be reached at Msmelimedina@gmail.com

Janel Cloyd

is about the business of living her poems. She walks each step manifesting verbs and leaving her words everywhere she goes. Her work appears in the Cave Canem digital anthology, Gathering Ground. She is published by the Yellow Chair and Poeming Pigeon. She is a Watering Hole fellow. Currently, she is completing an artist residency with the Willow Arts Alliance.

Flora Montes

was born and raised in the Bronx. She is an Entrepreneur and is the CEO of Bronx Fashion Week. She put her writing voice on hold for a few years while bringing her dream of a Fashion House to life to the beautiful borough of the Bronx and making history. Rediscovering her writing through this writing workshop feels like going back to her first love. This is her first published poem in over a decade.

Sydney Valerio

is a Bronx native and resident that enjoys focusing on the socio-cultural aspects of life that shape our perspective. She dedicates her 'gift to uplift' to education, youth development and the preservation of cultural literacy. In 2015, she joined the spoken word performance community as a member of the Full Circle Ensemble. She has performed in the National Black Theater, The Bronx Museum of the Arts and most recently, her one woman show "Matters" sold out at The Nuyorican Poet's Cafe. Visit her website www.sydneyvalerio.com to access her published poetry and event announcements.

Jama Clark

currently works in advertising and is the co-founder of a group called History Making Beauties. The group is composed of women who inspire others through their heroism, radiance, and positive impact on social and environmental change. Jama has been the keynote speaker at multiple events and also works as a freelance voice actor. She has always written but was most recently driven to write by the loss of her father however she was given the strength to share her gift by the women that have embraced her. Continually giving back to the people and organizations that have changed her life, Jama is currently writing a book that she knows will inspire women to choose courage over fear.

Jama Clark dreams of sitting across from Ava Duvernay and the amazing story teller Rutina Wesley while creating a series based on the many stories she has written based on the women that have inspired her. Jama would love to perform her work on stage one day and with her creative talent and beautifully powerful speaking voice the sky is the limit. Jama Clark can be reached historymakingbeauties@gmail.com.

Peggy Robles-Alvarado

is a resilient tenured New York City educator, a CantoMundo, Academy for Teachers and Home School Fellow as well as a two time International Latino Book Award winner and author of Conversations With My Skin and Homenaje A Las Guerreras/ Homage to the Warrior Women. As an initiate in the Lukumi and Palo spiritual systems, Peggy uses her experiences and her incredible rhythmic energy to challenge social taboos, celebrate womanhood and honor cultural traditions. She is a 2014 BRIO performance poet award winner and in 2016 she was named one of the 25 Most Influential Women of the Bronx, a BCA Arts Fund and Spaceworks Bronx Community Artist grant recipient. Peggy has been published in 92Y's #wordswelivein, NACLA, The Center for Puerto Rican Studies, and The Bronx Memoir Project. She has been featured on HBO Habla Women, Lincoln Center Out of Doors, Poets and Writers Connecting Cultures Reading, and The BADD!ASS Women Festival. Peggy is continuously creating and supporting literary events through Robleswrites Productions and is currently pursuing her MFA in Performance and Performance Studies at Pratt Institute. Her latest book The Abuela Stories Project debuted December 2016 at The Bronx Museum of the Arts. For more information please visit Robleswrites.com.

                              Listen

                              to your

                              spirit

whisper to blood   body   and bone then go

                              write

                              your

                              story

#magicmakingisnotforpendejas
#letthemcallyourname
#letthemfindyou
#legacy

www.ingramcontent.com/pod-product-compliance
Lightning Source LLC
Chambersburg PA
CBHW020210090426

42734CB00008B/1009